THINK OF THE DANGER

THEA BROWN

THINK OF THE DANGER

H_NGM_N BOOKS

www.h-ngm-nbks.com

FIRST H_NGM_N EDITION, 2016

ISBN-10:
0-9903082-5-1
ISBN-13:
978-0-9903082-5-6

book design & cover artwork / Heidi Reszies

For a complete listing of titles, or for more on this book, visit:
www.h-ngm-n.com/think-danger

TABLE OF CONTENTS

III.

IV.

I.

HELLO: A TREATISE, ENTREATY

To nothing, in particular
they say (I say) a window into briars.
I say (you say) we are heading
into a woods at night—a green
space full of cedars where hangs
a single incandescent chandelier,
crystal, from the tallest fir
in the middle dark. They say this
is memory, I say this is (very)
fancy or a charm to ward off
the like, you, the chandelier illuminates
only immediate surroundings, though
coin-eyed owls perch nearby.
When it rains the crystal prisms shudder,
but careful moss baffles the sound.

ECHOLOCATION

—

Despite all efforts, I can't find who invited me to this party, though the houseplants are phenomenal: jades and mother-in-law tongues and violets in white and a pale ivy I can't name. I reel from room to room, never settling. Everything upholstered in beige velvets and sage corduroys, floral tapestries bearing bright peonies, or maybe they're bee balm. How do I know? Outside lightens. I search for an exit.

—

On the black wall opposite the basement stairs, a buck's head peers out the half window above the sink to the artifactual garden in back. Angular sculptures crafted of chromed farm equipment. It's dawn, now—the pinks are pinking, the blues milky ere solidifying to their daytime regimen. The rust in the yard refuses all glinting. There is no sound. I find your letter in a hatbox and read:

> But can you see this, can you see this electricity? By which I mean, of course, my internal lights. Pull back your gaze from the tractors and spade and tell me—what do you

think? My lights help me carry you. O, my contemporary
future. They say, The future will look back on this (Ahem)
As something (Ahem!) Splendid!

The glass out back is blinding, exposed in its
viable utility. By sunset, it'll crack.

RUBY THE VISIBLE

The droplets gemstones overgrown, skin soaked and smooth, single glints.
The facets, all slopes enclosing hermetic red forward, unsearchable.
Pulses warm light past the ringed horizon, direction every
level glow like ember in the air around the blooms, no garden.
Remember: said gem red cannot be hidden or dismantled by sunlight,
only obscured. Though sunlight can be obscured,
the sun does not hide itself. Redder and most sun-like
borne inside the body, as blood
makes its own light otherwise. Boils
waterways as an additive but not the blood.
Asterism glanced at an angle bends the living
stream, which yet continues guided by its vessels.
Circulation security in one's own will to
dispel bad dreams, like fire, like vision when the systems run
smoothly streaming regardless forward.
The horizon circles and eddies pattern the paths,
hidden though not by choice, identifiable signals
in the mood for it. A ruby palmed in the pocket as protection
the next best thing to a ruby tucked under the tendons on
the inside of the wrist, disguised as biologic though the crystal itself
impenetrable by blood. The last threads of
orange facing the stars of the dark dome above.
Blood sings around the obstruction, forever passing.

CANDLE MOUNTAIN PINE

In a dark stage, this endless
Chatter, a mechanism for coping or
A cover for melancholy. Trickery either
Way and not enough to drink. Considering
All I've left tied to the tracks, a swift exit
Sounds like right medicine, stage left.
Call when you land, land where you fall,
Starched celestial, star-shaped shroud
In a diamond field—unquarry your best feelings
And sell them for a bite.

CARRIAGE HORSE

A lake in a city, all reflection fast
To the weather, deliberate shores.
A glass for the carriages, a brighter
Vision, lights doubled back to the eye.
The horses all balk, individual moments
Of collapse seldom seen on the street.
An aerial vision, utilitarian to the face.
The unicorn's north, through the weave
Of the city, this home left to molder
For matte golds. The compass spins
Or jerks. The horse's legs go stiff,
The tongue dries, manure.
This is all wrong. The dogs circle,
One dies.

More mockery poor horse, waxing
A nothing reverie to a snarl, a star
Striking trees, fields, fervent in
Revelry, fervent praise, eleven days
Of nothing. Detail a process, detail
Your agency—bodyless, bottomless.
Screws all tightening, water rising,
Stippled, verbal. The park devours
Its brood, returns to sleep another night.

DIAMOND FULL SPECTRUM

The petals gemstones overgrown, stem heavy and mirror, single glints.
Lavender edges the pools, garden clarity or translucence in a sky heavy today,
collecting more sky from the south and pulling it to the oncoming comet, waiting
as bright white spins to bright gray. All colors ground down and reconstituted,
still to be found in prisms. Gold and silver bearers of, fidelity fixed. So said
the diamond, carbon, pinned to the left arm in gold, weathering provides
like the life it is, dispenses impractical fortitude in the face of longing to be otherwise.
So said though such purity, pulsing through the band gold enclosing intention,
less cool, instead focused within the circle reveals the colors contained
within otherwise white light. And this, maybe, clear focus, white hot for some.
The fox's tail as it retreats, trots from messy leaf rustle oncoming, decaying,
a bobbing single patch of white. If a diamond more crystal than clear,
then clarity obscured by colors, by mood, becomes headier and optional
as a reason to focus. Mulch smell breeds, does not deter, pulls closer.
When the diamond coaxed from the earth pulls in light, it becomes
closest to the heart and stomach.

EAGLE TYPE LIGHTLINE

Closest the pier, a city in blank
constancy, sequoias in six months,
a sixth moth, this month
to chill later's coastal calendar.

Living as a scientist, my fever glasses
fogged, fevered light in a haze, hazy full
lighted skill, celebratory glowing
filmed in frost or cloud. Waders ghost

gone in a hazy shore cloud strung
from lamp to lamp. Holiday goes pinging
through cables and wading proves
singing now, sandy engineering

with sand in all the bottles and
beaches not meaning anything
but watery. So passenger a wintry rain
with fill to coast-like mothscape, quiet

microscoping, moths like owls as light
like owls as a future like fine, white
to season a frost full as quiet, or repeated
quieter, less the waders gone home.

I ran then, a tern, I ran collecting light
strung file-like, strung fabled in street fair,
the city staggering up and around like an iceberg
in sand. My glasses fevered in haze in rime

light, ground halting minus sparking
a blue-red green or sand in falling or
moths from seascape circling strung
cables, light-emitting, holiday hazy

or not, or they shut
down at night. For partly owls
or less guidance. Or shimmery still,
for pretty-making, in all the breakers.

A BANK OF WINDOWS

These small boxes exist to be filled with images, or oranges, or shore noise, or orcas. Lastly bathing from the ship's deck, from the life raft, to problematize, the projections must fill a prophesy, fit quietly in an emergency.

Everything on this list means to confuse me to forgetting my intent in its creation and so far, a few items ticked, but not by me. Last week you spoke everything in the miniature solar system, and tomorrow I'll go to the shore to build you an ovation worthy of such information. Where the cliffs fall comes and

goes. You know, I used to

act. To say out loud to oneself in ocean grass where is my heart where is my heart is a terrible habit but only thinking it is maybe a little better, though not something to be often felt in wading.

SAPPHIRE, BODY VOICED

The bear a gemstone overgrown, tracing the light and the sky, through viewing.
This play'd been writing itself for days before the generator burned out
—clanging keys a stranger medium. A public Bruce Spruce, a bow
on a sailor, velvet, a Gibson. A small acknowledgement
to soften the distance: nod, wink, tear.

Bent and stutters, blue light unpinched. The diving bear captive,
beat now shatter. Bubbles, a plume, a thought. Hand to glass,
fixed to muzzle, breaking back to retreat. Surface spun white.
Spectators whistle, streamers unfurl—
to deaden the cheers: sink, sunk, sank.

PROXY

Calendrical reversals, all calamity aside. All murder as drama: product callous, product calculated. World clock halts, tacks forward two, reverses one, settles. All eyes ice. All listening, rounded. Blackbirds, listening. All eyes twice, closing and was the passing quiet at least, like peeling transparency from a screen, bulb still bright. Blackbirds on wire sign nothing, no pulse; grounded no mind through cable, no candle left burning, melt tapping slow inhale, no static just cutouts: policeman, fireman, medic. Hillside tinder a blip. Was the passing what finally held you in calm or resignation and worry forgotten. To forget to be frightened, a last lost.

THE ALTERATION OF STRESS CHARACTERISTICS

the art of edifice
efficacy of artifice
aesthetics of stop
please and show me
how you're thinking
through this still
space with scope
and scale—
it's huge as bees
shot from a cannon
my sentences
are choked
by facts, now
pay attention this
is very personal:
a one-shot pelican
harbinger of coast

ABLE AMBLING EGO SHIFT

A pistol through cheek in the floral sense, the florid sense, in the new means dominating social technology. It's not that nature alienates us, it's that we make it technology's province and demand explanation furthering our network. Can we not understand a pistol through the cheek? Can we understand flowering?

A poison pit flowers out in my esophagus.
It is the shape of a tiny tree, like a dogwood.
Its petals signal something new. Something like ___

It means what happens when I take the dog out at night. He sniffs and stares into the lamp-lit park, dark with danger, and I stare there too. And while we're both staring I hear a rustling and look up and there, there are hundreds of long-silent crows, thick as nigh-lit storm clouds. They've absorbed everything. They're waiting to descend.

EMERALD THE HEART CHAKRA

The yard a gemstone overgrown, terracotta split and violet, firewheel.
About limitless impossible—no good on the fly
and the natural world contained in steamy, seamless glass.
Ornery space collapses to expectations as exceptions; read: meteors.
All accepted by exception doesn't mean that I'm astrologically inclined.
And really one *would* rather, so rearrange all crystal objects
clockwise to encourage the afternoon light to button itself up more quickly.
Calmly, afterward, world nothing everything cycles eye-close, bright,
too much too close, enclosed, but yes I do not want but in
what direction of all those available, no, I don't.
One would rather impossible closures, new leaves tucked behind new ears and soft.
The leaves ought to be gilded, growth clipped or else how to observe
with real feeling without baubles. In other instances: Is it all right to
smash the glass and pull the fire alarm because I want to go home.
Is it all right to saw and pull dead branches from the willow
through the window, strings of leaves swaying like kelp,
because it's said to cast a green evil eye otherwise.
Is it all right: too eyes, two close, forgets it, *it*, meaning *all*.
Everything. Ever already uploaded for later. Yes, a future memory.
Ever lose local control of the hands, but in what, from what angle?
My information is personal and worthless and I'd like to keep it that way
so I can be careless with it, as though worth and care ever aligned right.
I am working over all the forest I've found and know still more I won't,
I don't want to understand. Of course the heart is green.
Mostly smoothed edges, all growth.
I see it all again just, like the first time.

ALL MY BAD DREAMS COME TO THE PARTY

Sometimes it's too loud next door, the reverb,
Standalone. The walls begin to shed their designs.
In the past they flew into my mouth. They clambered,
Stuck. Paisley. A border of roses. A Joan Mitchell print.
Mostly I dream of a bloody nose, though last
Night it was bats. Iron-y ribbons, red and silver
Empty silos, steel sky pin droplets, the blood
Running into my mouth. I found this shiny
In the garbage, I said. A ruby and gold. And then a car
Comes with a thump. There's no tone in my nothing,
Though last night it was bats, locked in the safe house.
I've got a quarter that'll get you halfway to Gravity Hill,
You told me. I'll need it. I was locked in there with them.

II.

HI! I AM A MACHINE.

Not really. Hello! I am a machine in a landscape.
Still no. I am a machine and a landscape. Probably also
False. But that and you—both machines. That one is silent
And still. A smooth box bearing dull reflections like granite.
It has no seams, but a solitary, blue light and a wire, copper,
Leading from a corner through your hand to that tree over there.
It's an oak tree. No. It's a simple maple, too thin for any real use.
You are both the machine and I think this is stupid because it is
Romantic and there's no time or space for that behavior here.
This arboretum works its days on a pulley system.
When the sun comes up the box will blink On or Off,
Depending. But either way, you will wake.

CLEANING UP THE VERBAL SITUATION

you are   terrified
we are also   terrified, terrific
there, the smell of wildfires
there, the smell of well water
what are there are what are those
smells: a crisis of privatization
we can't know—increasingly
we understand our words
as we hear them we are
increasingly private: crisis, silent
the smells and social use, mine
the industrialization finally
disintegrates let's construct
some together time: an underwater
ride: this is not addressing you
this is addressing a finite significance
your intimacy is such that I'd like
yours, truly

THE BRONZE REGION SITS UP THE HILL IN A POCKET OF SMALLER HILLS

O, this tempered practicality, faceted for purchase of green birds,
Displays of golden affection in the equinoctial suburbs. Dew rockets morning
Light like diamonds, the grasses all dip and shake off the burden.
When the sugarcane runs low, a gem-cutter suffices, though the substitution lacks
A certain something, a zing, an angular spark. You're such a *shipyard* sometimes, you
Tell your friend who's more like your brother, Your vervanity cuts loose really
At the most inconvenient moments. D'hivernage in the water supply, he says,
A Cyprus in every yard, a Suburban parked by chainlink. Don't think you're special
And all this time Guadalupe's pollen collection swells dangerously in the medicine cabinet.

MIDWESTERN

Objects alchemize or metal to a shrift, catching
Full aversion in dust pile-up, sandstorm bubbling
Through the window, reluctance virtue in the sun
Setting, a wilder population come to root out evil.
The comet roving closer, elliptical firestorm—too easy
In worship, the farmhouse a perfect frame absorbing
Destruction's dispatch. Give up that face already.
No notice, tawny portraiture from the butcher's bed
Casts a pale in the striped hallway, perhaps a pail
For harrowing night flames, gaslit in mercurial mirrored
Glass. Darkens. Hear it? Rumble low through the yearlings,
Poised in up-sniff ready, flashed out at second glance.
A glacier's timeline re-sketched in gale, crops kneel
To the word. This is what the rocking chair moves for,
Wildly unnatural, chains in the cellar strung for airlock.
Do we know what it is to drape, to frame? Fuller biding,
Fuller menace, sepia web vibrates a full minute before
Halting like a charm. The lake shrugs, pulls back, opens
Its center like all the plain's throat. Full minutes in
Arriving, generous acceptance, sea-like provisions
In a kind-of-sail churning power, halting current,
Rustling stalks, stopped. Just the rumble. You see it,
Come closer.

TIRE FIRE WITH STILL LIFE

Today's breathing includes benzene from the landfill fire, the tire fire
They call it in the papers. To abdicate leisure time, call the currents:
Filtered limeaid, too much TV, party drinks in the afterroom or keep it
Limited, roar, no parachutes. The outdoors, pouring cycle keeps
A cache of windswept, whirring, vibration in revolutions to
Powerback the grid, skelter occupied the mainmast or pillar. Post?
Built to a spec visible on interstates, trailer beds, blades like the curvature
Of modernization itself: precise and bland, transport reckless. Shots all
The way up, to the blade edge peeling out to suffer the word, to repeal
Resignation at industry's compilation. The sun won't glint in beauty's last
Day. Glint's for continuance, glare for slipshod sure finale. No one's ready.
When the earth powers itself, we have all gone to sleep in a year in
Which there weren't minions, or there were but come on. Living's a blast.
Stoke the plume, kill it faster. Transpose independence with leukemia,
Buffalo gnats with stampede, herd with thunder. It's all pretend—
An almost-moon in the news cycle, byline and all.

THE NEXT TOWN OVER

sees itself in our revitalization, commercials,
layer cakes, lined, iced on counters and fortified
or glaze cracked, or waiting all reflects gem settings,
platinum lever pulled and bevy leveled, brick cracks
coyly through the quartet's set, like please try again, *please*
again, facilitated access in other words, green-lit then
lost sight, tracking every dot's point dotting pleasantest
paths across in living moral—familial teaks, the ever-crowd
calling, *cover softly*—in tonight's dream we are all over
in the canopy, fruit-sated and -filled, we are blood-related and
I pull a seashell from bark, nestled, an insect constructed
like dead leaves blends impressively into the trunk
before me—and compresses us more by unbecoming
easy and refinancing a color that forever, forward emanates

CONCEAL BY VIRTUE OR CONQUEST

I think my research into the effects of new media
On the existence of audience as proxy for self is important.
I think yours is too. In other words, we are all important
As a unit. The thing is, I do want your prayers, I do want
A little donkey and some myrrh mixed into my martini.
You are my favorite little prayer—have I told you? An introvert's
Hoarding affection for panic only leads to nights in the hole.
There are so many things I want to show you! My collections,
My collections of collections, my collections of desires,
My catalogues of chrysalises, grape popsicles stuck to
Tongues I've had in mine own mouth only once. Or twice?
Or imagined. What's the etiquette? Don't go to third unless
You're willing to lick everyone? Everyone watches for the myth
Arc and everyone experiences the small revelations as pivotal
To character identification in the grand scheme. Everyone
Trusts. Or not, in which case we're watching with a squint
And that's fine too. There's so little left to reveal. But today
There's agency or agencies, unravel. Individual actors within
The audience. Spread your love and part your digits. Speak
Your nothing into a well of clambering budgies all pecking
At the cereal box in the corner. Some day, it'll talk back.

THE DREAM

Wonder mumbles or something like I like that, there.
Dusky imprecision flaunts the better half like charm
Links reticence to daze—all the jokes saving all the lonely
Militant hi there. You're something, not charming, and why
Take up hands against? The dreams come back: black Escalades,
Spray of knuckles through tint. Go forward, go forward,
We can't be sure though hear that hiss? Residual line
Tap exhale or breeze amongst poplars, cherry blossoms.
Registers a sigh of slow surveillance. The dreams come
Back of everyone set to play in the wings and hush.
The empty amphitheater, trickle mist through slats meant
For off-gas. The swamp leaves trails to us all and the flags
Signal forward, we are dispersed. My heart's homestead
A reckoning, fogged pier. What to make of the monuments
Lighted like jewelry and just as warm. The hand does not reach
Across for all its waiting, anticipation mistake, for naught,
Smoke screen no screen after all. The rivers cut everything off.
Black Escalade, go forward. In the steady, slow humidity, everything
I love shudders off.

GALLERY

Into a new medium, left without guide but the line undecayed, falls
Back behind treading to entrance. Fruit flies twitch approval
Along the line's path, make for hazy calibration, each jostle
Registers data collection, points to plot on the disturbance chart
I keep bedside beside water jar, keys, skull. Thought marred by the line,
Now fastened to cup and webbed, an indignity to be sure but fanciful still,
This deafness. In the narrative of horizon breaking out morning, the line
Taught and curving out means a limit either nonporous or
Imaginary. An arrow travels the path undetected, whir of feather
Caught only by air. The facility's temperature is important: The needle
Jumps above a mark, signals discomfort, decomposition, or nothing.
Fine blue line set against panic as concept. As actionable, instantiate.
Graphs a twitch history worth charting. Worth mention.

WHAT ELSE IS

Does it mean we look only either forward or back, imagine.
Both all the time and divorce from the earth of it improbable,
The promontory. Cast gaze, cat's tongue. Look out. The earth
Pulls prey from nestle to a waiting gullet. Bloody bright, and
Help again. For softening. For single track once on the inside.
Choice drops out of the equation stabilized. I do think because
I have to. Eat and eat and eat and then. Watch the forest
Scenery converge to a point in infinity into the bank of trees.
Blue green. Does it mean we are carried. Away to a memory, thin
As crepe paper with none of the party. Streamers not streamed
Means it's tomorrow already, and for whose celebration? All
Film coats tile, blood spatter. Tile over, the forest grows
Large and full consumption, like a belly. Like the dark in there.

REGRETS

I am not young and I can no longer attend your party; correction
: I can no longer attend any parties, but especially not this one—
yours—any one that involves sitting not facing a window or door
and waiting for a signal. Here's what happened:

We have lowered myself to the floor. We have deposited
myself on my porch, under the swing. We have drunk myself
from the hose. Forward flick, bluedark pinned to chest's cavern.
Of ___X___ all, ___X___ quiet. I carry no photographs unless

IDs count because I love discriminately. Oh yes, your party is the worst.
Every angle, three times, and the echo never alters, aches right.
Not reproduction, just altered remembrance. Your party is one of these
___X___. Its edges do not become soft over time,

do not degrade. I can no longer attend. Tree splits after
the storm, not during. We have already delivered myself home.

Vastly different form

THE GRECIAN HOTEL

An island resort with a view from the Meadow Suite, a song
for amaranth from 10th story windows, thrown Thracian vigil,
grown sinful in breakfast. This croissant's been fruit-filled
with dryad technology yet my wave sallies forth, jonesing
for greyhounds, a citrus-y hair for the runway cut short.

The elevator's stuck between 7 & 8. It always gets like this here.

To finish the season, tuxedoes appear and the hotel bar runs
full-packed with glamour, with lifesavers and UV lights,
with autographed fancy. How to say nothing while building
a bridge? Alternate light patterns, make pretty a thing.
Kill revelers and holidays with buckets of joy.

title poem in 2nd section

THINK OF THE DANGER

every evening, songbirds
settle in the oaks, passive in
all of that

think of the danger, you out there
for you, every morning color rings
the same, thinking of little danger
birdsong, some dark sounds rolling
in, your perfect meadow's lost
its dew for fear of bluster wrath, think
of your family, think of singing

back here, little birdsong, doleful like
your little sister eats a little coconut, gets
prepped for surgery, darker now culls daffodils
from fruit stands, irons her hair, pulls it

out, you! little lightning, little storm cloud, iron
swift 'cross daisy fields, think
of all the little caterpillars calling out not
enough, not enough! kill your image!
get it dead! hangdog dogdead!

little lightening, show your firework
philharmonic excess! the empty sky is
full of light and light is full of fill, reflective
materials or reflection radiating lightways,

immediately accessed and gilt
framed, heaving lively under fields full
of quaint wild life

but think
of
the
danger

think of the danger, think of it thinking like your
wonderstorm broke heavy
this time, left fractured glass,
dazed parakeets, reinvigorated
like frozen well water, like buckets
of rain, like silver ocean
mist that rises and rises
toward black pockets of sky

IN A BLAZE THIS LANDSCAPE'S UNPRODUCTIVE FOR ANALYSIS

You wouldn't know where you are. You take your name—what fate attends,
Where it leads as the ink glues. Mountains spill from icy lakes just like promised on
The screen next door, the entire fire a moment in excess. Your heat to you is terrain,
Called pleasant, recalled. A cavalcade of walnut trees lines the foreground,
Reduces access. When you lie to you it makes you appear weak and capricious
Though you generally get what you want anyway. Glug goes the terrain, you fall into
A dream while talking to you on the computer phone. You are asking a lot
Of questions about climbing and trickery. You could work up a sweat just lying there.
It doesn't have to mean anything.

WHAT HAPPENED LAST NIGHT

What is it about the exposition?
A man peers out his window, invested.
My vision goes pink as a sunset.
There are so many ways for me to tell you about it.
The one I pick will make a difference, small but fatal.
Then, picking home from the display, a root catches my ankle,
Mangles the skin, thin strings of red down the pale,
Like time rain's retreating crackle, trail of glimmer through smoke.
A sulfur settling 'cross town, citronella at the ready.
It's hard to feel a thought when the center gives or never arrives
Or when the no takes hold, blank face, blank or everything.
You are drunk and weepy, chrysanthemum evoking
Childhood lawns, adult lawns, the lost response, delayed.
You pinch your nose and the finale obliterates all memory
Building for the time being. Nothing happens over
And over again and we settle in, we settle.

EXPOSURE

for J.L.

—

Yesterday at the beach, this too on the nose. A rainbow
umbrella, soda in glass, dunes collapsing sightless
into the lake, newly clear. The algae declines,
the prey fish decline, the mussels flourish. Everyone takes
pictures of the water with their smartphones, spreading
the new clarity's effect to those farther from shore.

—

How does meaning slip away like it does? Seeping through
memory's rust? The basement heater's corroded seams pulse
heavy water to a drain in cement. Mineral buildup adds its mass
but does not stop the leak. To where? Does the hand on fire
lose its urgency, stagnated to image?

—

A simple comfort, yes, but Jim says some of us, exposed to an exploding star, burst to cloud, hover near enough to be recognized as causal, while others remain intact but fly off endlessly one way. Encountered later on their routes, their trajectories may be traceable both directions but not immediately accessible as reason. There is no space

—

for intention here. A simulated scorched-film setting intensifies the weather in retrospect, a memory of the beach left to peel in the sun. Waves recede, mussels go lakeward, unpeopled scenery a winsome effect. Today a gull pecks at the remnants of picnics, but tomorrow the sun will rise and rise until nothing is left.

WHEREFORE EDITS, HOWSO LIGHT?

—

When you tried to call you yesterday you heard you breathing. What you said in there: I've got the bad fores, but what happened to the limelight calling? What happened to the monthly Armageddon report? We're into the year now.

—

All's clear for May with blue days, light rain, sprouted basil. A new fuchsia hanging basket for the porch, floating like your loyalties are roving—you see them, but you don't care. The finches keep rebuilding their clover nest after removal from the basket and you read that man ate 80% of that other man's face and didn't even bother to kill him first. They didn't even know it, thought he was dead. You came to this place for solace, an alternate gateway. Beaches and sunsets, say what you want: ferris wheel, churned margarita, boardwalk, fence, candy light. Two men, one with tattoos, both with beers, facing away from the waves, watching the waitress bring nachos. Not enough gas to get you down the coast by nightfall. The answer's Christmas Eve dinner in a diner in Modesto or easy saturation, lights in the storefronts, everywhere the carousels.

—

Sometimes you do feel like the first commercial spaceship delivering supplies to the International Space Station, retrieving experiments and god knows. Silent you, all blue about the gills, knocking on the plexi. Credentials matte like blacktop against the screener. You've never tried the rides for larking, only stood slack-jawed at the chain-link, eyeing death peals from the teacups and worse. The map's all folded in on itself and your memories pile in front of you, insurmountable clutter, gadgets, wrenches, funny mirrors, etc.

—

The CDC issued a statement: No zombie virus. Well. Add that to the pile, fluttering breezy mess. Who even knows what antigravity medical research is? What came back from out there in what cargo holds through hostile environs? What ecosystem? It's like the landscaped boardwalk of the universe with colorized off-gassing out there. You read that woman ate her baby's toes and part of its brain. What else? News cycle revelries don't tell you what to do, how to hunker like you do. This getaway's a scam, but at least a happy one. You pull together your own worst ideas. You reassure you it's massing that makes memory last. Memories like this one.

TODAY WE'RE ON VACATION

for L.J. & J.K.

—

We travel through a terminal, meeting a dull train to pull us toward the city. Unimpressed by our research technology, the city glides by like a dancer in heaving display. Our equipment, sensitive as it is, escapes through a window toward grassy beacons—dials whirring, tickers ticking. The wildlife shatters. We don't follow, but continue toward the dunes. The circling birds tell us we're close. On the shore, we meet a kid taking focused measurements:

—

But let's not to the universal, elliptical mess, you say to no one in particular. A fogged coastline, edged specific—a mind traveling out to the boundaries of worldscope for travel. A spinning analogy to bring in the known. You point at the empty highway behind us. This lighthouse's unstable, thistle mist ecclesiastical and if this is a place to go then go there, you say. The webbing between pores a reminder of give. My slack face obliges, behavior otherwise unsavory.

Goodbye, Science, your arctic research will have no place in this future. Parrot authority, here is your arctic diet: *A seal is a just a bear that has adapted itself to sea life*. I will concern myself with the self only until the trees running the boulevard spark themselves to witness in the fall.
An ungenerous eye to crystalline power lines. Telephone cables never tell a story like satellites but for charred fawns caught from failing raptors.

—

Our ever-present frontier future glimmers and quiets as history blues its edges in shadow. The sun sets. In six months, a stirring and the city

looms skeletal and lush in invitation unstated. Everyone is awake but silent.
A streetlamp flickers in the Inner Sunset as we look for something
to kill and eat. We work our fingers into sidewalk chamomile
and bring them to our mouths. A

Folly? In retreat, we take in the city from the summit.
Is this voyeurism old fashioned? Have its resources depleted?
We have abandoned our mission and geography. We breathe grandiose
nonetheless. The outdoor plants here bloom without nurture, so many
times a poppy breaks open. The fog pulls in and the peninsula, a still
sloping into—all bridges all edgeless and we pass into wake.

SUMMER WORD AS FIELD

—

It used to be modern reforestation or nautical mapping, a gallery
pinning caught branches to shifting liminal confluence, a peacock
at the summer home at the sea and when you returned, I remembered
how small and relentless sealight, its case for composure, there
a possibility toward facts fused, a widow's walk; there were nights
I tried to sleep early but kept up to the looking for a greenish light
of re-emergent insistence, twine of every color one binds to a shore.

—

As measured response we'll will to fullness our residual
opulence, a composition of so many notes it drowns
this picture I've endlessly scripted, binding nights and after
the split, if I took you for a doctor would you bend to the work
with precise defiance, rough-handedness while I prattle
a situating narrative, anchored through rising starlight, seaming
landscapes like patchwork; a means of forgetting creation myths.

—

Shorebirds have taken to the porch, again.

—

Lately in conversation your role stutters to provide a backdrop against which I am aging
and so the fleas nibble, flea, there're formal elements between our utterances, to fancy up
the phrase, pretty-up you, there's only so much difficulty per distance and it is
deceiving, this summer, who's reciting last facts, those upon which memory sits
storing heft for histories; it's not far as validity falters glamorously in light reflected
from watercolors, a setting precise in horizon, prairie's exhaustion around a fire

built from sitting room combustibles. In other words, this is not exactly where
we meant to be by and now, this dream has lead to
regeneration, and there's a ticking in all
my bureaus, my beau, I'm terrified of wildlife.

RUEFUL DILETTANTE, FULL OF FEELING

In the sense of geography, we can't help this I as it stands, listing
Toward the backyard, the woods beyond, a wall overtaken by ___

___

To circulate worldly romance, if it is romance, substitute concatenation in parable
To rewrite endtimes, like yesterday the dogs came back, wresting sentiments
Contained as cordates, fell splintering to a faltered foundationalism, repeated
An abyss of catastrophe or possession and apostrophe, this willful execution
Of strongfield, heart donors, contain us! We won't sleep still.

All of this to call to mind fragmentary irony, an inability to erase selfward
Beating body biography, meaning memory proof, meaning building a mind
As hunger struggles withholding, redefining two truths, facestarred
Rational, truthscience as a chemistry containing levels clear to newness
Unlike splitting substance, what's happened to wellstored water, kenneling.

They breed, split irrational, untrue building fast containment, boundaried
History swells in the imagined real, unhappened, full of rhyming, practice
Feeling practice feeling practice historical nostalgia, uncomfortable closeness
To recalled misinformation. And now the dogs came back and now the wall is
Complete in its disintegration. We, luck lost to empty fields. We, the full
Heartsore, bled out along a fence.

THE DAILY DAILY

The creek bed
curves ahead, cluttered

in a morning rising
toward rosing as fog

burns off the rivers.
Dry for a season, one's dark

always better wavers,
better than rousing two's,

rather winding one
and pressed against

the flat blue. Today, a
wisp and flattening.

One, today, a winner's
panting lack of palm to

waist, lacking stitch
-spent wind setting

ornamental grasses to
tilted reverence in day

light. Two battling winded,
balking stutter, one's

oxygen-rich heart rallies
in heat, palpitates and threats

surface all around, rising
like stealth gray Escalades and

disappearing to destroy
another man's woe and lack,

weave and bobbing buoy.
One's yesterdays written

up into the vault's
mouth, cool and dust.

Two attacked, brought
back to the living in

a spin of wind, a memorial's
red eyes blinking.

The longer the yearn pulls
hardest to forgetting. All

the backward, all of it
backward, all of it and years

roll back past a horizon made
pink by the setting, the end

-less peel. All the clicks in one
and two, the locks clacking

into place behind one's
looking back. One, the path

a splitting line. Two,
the path, a rising dust.

SHADE FOUND

for M.B.

The problem with now is I can't ever
Remember its happening. Sitting on

The truck hood, rude thoughts,
Sunset on the watershed. A flea song,

Skitter around back. All the problems pile
Up, remain clear, decompose to a tune.

Black water torrential night and day,
What's a dirty dog to do? Head into

The disco, quiet-up now according
To the flyaways. You never get lonely,

Only old and new. Because the sun
Scorches the truck, red paint peels and we do

Look fine here, ticking like engines in the shade.
How me and you eat those melting chocolates,

Slow. If only the flies were buzzing
A little louder, the sun setting a little

Later. Summer's superfluous bonfires.
Fall a welcome respite rightly,

Else the neighbor's raccoon posse,
All eyes in the headlights.

But what cares now. What, indeed.

WEDDING GREENS

I am wandering through an English hedge maze
in California. Thank you for understanding.
White roses just overbloomed.

Clover creep and spade leaf, bony body vineyard
with orderly vines strung up
chest high.

Gusts giggling in guests' ears, in the bridal party's
endless careless poses. Settled dark dirt, rich
and full of potential,

under grapes green reflected in roses below,
the next lower row, blossoms bear
milky fists.

Breezes more cinematic relief across the lawn,
the third row, lowest for redundant
seeding

afar, aclose, a grim grid, monochrome green.
By teen green mean like
the inside

of a music box minus the dancer. The details only
seem tedious during their nascency,
never worry.

Men who never learned how to talk to women without
children. Lawn like a living room,
contained

to yawn. To be bored more unapologetically.
Less childlike than other circumstances,
the lawn like

the sea like a meadow and a sea but not yellow.
Green posing by the green inside the pool of
a stone fountain.

Guests mosey when instructed. Flutes, tumblers,
rocks abandoned everywhere. Someone else will
clean this up, from now on.

GO

hey, a fair analysis of complete blood
counts, becomes

one, individual of such analyses
of we are all moving

ticks green across a black screen

into and out of our living,
parameters defined some
-times by nothing at all but
a flash before weather

leaves a negative map
for wild surroundings

not so nihilist in the woods, then
stillness becomes more than

one becomes mutagenic, my
my epiphanies, heart-leaf

down the mantle over-and-again, fire

out and brick draft, heatless
and glib, to forest
plot outcomes of mood

on mortality, mood on matter, inky

splatter, mood as intra
-cellular activation back

/forth mainlines, virologic
when the option's harm

reduction reaction only, only
less, less harm sustained to

cells alone, all

when body's to blame
hey, cartographer, not so
carefully snuffed out, pull
back from danger like

pulling back gauze
to examine an opening,

bones bereft,
like drawing thin sheets

across bare legs, bare ready
avoiding new, all harm

becomes a tell,

susceptibility to infection,
access, osedax, or vision
toward new vista, stoplight
swinging while the populace swarms,

gesture toward gracious
before opening, index-to-thumb,

and acknowledging harm as that which
edges overspill, avoids, reduces

time dwelt in undergrowth
encroaching on the yard

and so see a sky dark dropping

instead, instead now
now, there and there, a forest
mulching itself into and out
of existence simultaneously

and so goes mindful death-mood avoidance
so skillfully perpetual as

seemingly sugar

dissolves in cold tea, as a whale

dissolving in the sea

I imagine my skull and how much more,

how reedy my mood becomes, momentarily so

removed from mortality, my

my mood undarkens, how

to avoid becoming my skull

reduce access to death by

opening, drawing

the fabric back, then drawing

back myself, pulling myself

back and opened, ob-

servant. Just we all are key,

us becomes, comes back,

and withdrawals.

CHALCEDONY, IN THE SUMMER CHAPEL

My ear a gate curled to spider frequency as dusk ripens to
a whirring—somewhere a top spins undisturbed, but here
Anjous and lilacs grow in through the windows, an instantaneous
illumination through petals—is it marble? A refraction?

You saw and collect the branches, raising your finger
to the still-burning village out to the west, its hovering image,
carameled smoke, in redirection of chimes ringing, of
charred brambles, of cinder drifting to the next open
plain, to dry moss in the intervals, to the worn chapel steps.

Again our summer's ruined, the wasted orchard singing
with fire. The chapel resounding, spiders darting from corners,
tracing their intentions from hideout to lookout in cobweb.
Sunset trickles in through the glass, spilling down the whitewash.

In the shingled house across the road, one clawfoot holds the sea,
the other a new planting of mint, relocated to quell invasive growth.
The orchard chatters, disappointing revelry, the perfect sunset of all
my dreaming. I never know what I'm hearing now. You hand me
your glasses and nod to the stained glass, but your far-sightedness tires me.

The ferrous cities out to the end of the path arrange themselves
around a single flowering tree. Inside, you cover your face with raw hands
and I make you a pear tart. I'm sorry about that. About the mint
and that we can no longer bathe. All the robberies.
Unempty terms, a blankness against something.

Quit your chapel farming, you, and quit your tiredness, your charts and seedrows. The spiders patrol the ceiling, chandeliers dropping periodically, choreography indeterminate. Vesper sparrow, how long can you bear this part of the country? Your mouth sputters forth, clumsy and clawing. You abandon your beacon, follow through the day.

CAMP

What morning, what mornings,
coarse red sand, knee-deep ocean,

bluffs below. To be windswept
all one's life, a biting drama,

a drama of erosion, particle scum
rings the pooled beach and sun

reddens, snaps, and fizzles then
bands of blue melt, striations

delicate above a rush of waves.
No fireflies.

A tiny white church and cemetery
face away from the somber ocean.

Backs to it. What salt rush:
rust. What listing. How to keep

speaking through it all. How
to set the tarp against the sky

above the grass and face
its opening west. How every

morning sun reveals the swarm,
all at once. How one blast could

sever the six-mile bridge. What
safety then. How the ocean

would buffer
the infection.

ESSAY: CALLING

—

with realism as a natural enclosure set against some sunset, event capture
as how real, perceptual, as in I understand you in your otherizing, you of my
Western acquaintance, of Western wagon trains and want for understanding
the other of knowledge like every day I think about going to the zoo every day
in my work clothes, grass-stained and torn at the elbows; an everyday carafe
careless in its blindness but can skepticism be a vocation? is it too soon

—

for the word possibility? like sometimes, there's repetition without meaning
or at least with consistency as realness, building the natural through doubt
in constructing a simultaneity of choices—constructs, even if choosing shores
up intention or to say you meant to visit the bison all along, to bypass
the tigers, you meant to call it a bison and it's called a natural surrounding or
a prairie, but we call everything we cross at a pitch, then bluestem, needle grass

—

fescue, galleta—if all the time we're talking about the relationship of art
to truth, we're talking about the way by which a sun is simultaneous, symbolic
and the primary force behind literal and non-literal systems of demonstration
and also this zoo is lovely as a space for our frontier and I've built a landscape
with bison for you or an other, a time still drafting objects as doubt is not

—

the same settling as skepticism, remember I would never leave you far
from this consideration of words, enactment toward knowledge, the fervent
work of frontier landscape construction; a time still with the understanding

of lightness, we approach a margin, we are approaching enactment, a trajectory over distance in observation, this natural enclosure of grasslands, to say we improvise through our doubt is adequacy or accumulation or acclimation

—

and a site of continuity, totalized empirical containment or enactment over a time still, what I'm trying to build right now is the middle plains and remember, I'd never leave you, my frontier through intention, acts of choosing time still, order resistance and a sentimental distance or simultaneity, massive astronomical units with objects belated, our frontiers as charred, a margin approach, a radical radial approach, this is what I'm calling it for you

Gertrude Stein-ish

FEVER ECOSYSTEM

—

is this an act of love or an attempted meaningful, meaning fevered
preservation of an other, meaning memory or meaning a mirror and isn't it
acute or like taxidermy, the remains of an impala killed by wild dogs, sun
bleached and waterless, this footage means our record here

—

but then again what a party this all turned out to be, heavy designs
signaled by upper lip, movements coordinated for a kill and we're having
quite a time here, actually we're killing it, our stats better than lions',
this recording

—

if it's always New Year's Eve, then there's always glitter stuck in the teeth
of endangered predators, and actually more compact documentaries
signal real danger, as people are dying over and over but keep diving
for underwater caves, places where salt and fresh waters merge to form
false skies, we're watching

—

the wild dogs, the caves issuing a plea, though the air is thick
with streamers, thick with hope to stop dying here or close these openings
for good, to say there is always a toast and sometimes celebration beside
these gaps, these parties and other kill locations, this need
for false skies, for record

IV.

HELLO THERE. HOW MANY TIMES ARE WE DOING THIS?

Let's get started:
It's ten thirty and once again
our inelegant hearts have turned
to tiny pelicans in our chests.
There's no way around some
states of ravenous collapse, so
let's focus, let's watch another
desultory parade of indulgences;
there's nothing else to do.
The pelicans beat their wings
inelegantly and devour pigeons
live, which we find disturbing
but really the problem is of
basic communication; a lack
of devouring images. We're after
an inventory of places the ocean
folds in secret pockets
because everyone's after
an inventory of ocean. But
the pelicans want more pigeons
and we tell the pelicans
to choke already. We'd like to see
tornados over water. That's right:
Be still, pelicans, you rank
cannibals—there's nothing you
can say for us right now.

HOME INVASION

—

Usually, I am
Stuck here between
Surrealists. Freudian?
Yes. Instinct? No.

The Dominion jars all
Hover around a dark point,
One-dimensional or endlessly
Dense, more disordered than
One at first considers.

The Dominion jars enclose
All similar points, one-
Dimensional and endlessly
Light.

—

In this system, this is my wonder:
A bat in the house, the kitchen, the bedroom, the study, the bedroom.
A bat in the house in the basement, a desperate chirping.
The bat multiplies and inhabits all dusky corners, upside down, rocking.
I crouch on the bed, still as a point.
The bed frame unmoors, bats bubbling and breaking and slushing against black walls as the whirlpool starts up again with the sound of a lawnmower.

A whale sounds.

It's true.

The space between wonder and terror is the intersection of dreaming and waking. Sounds simple, but you wait and see. Somewhere, a Dominion jar contains you in its glass.

THE LIGHT, THE HEAT

Little motion, your eyes pool reverie.
All this decorative melancholia in a silver fog
pacing loops around marble columns.
Whisper, moss, ghostly in the graveyard
no graveyard: slow on-ramp in rain.

Getting there forces contrition not felt in passing
though all up the lines go invisible in the slick.
We drive there because we said we would.
The light, the heat of that morning at the river,
every skiff decked for funeral, for revival,
final flagged coffins sent cheery into mist.

You are at odds with the core of your detachment.
Talking about it you reassure you the monster manifests
as your worst fear made tangible and tiny
but if your death fear's wasting, will the monster pace the decks,
peg-legged for showboating? Keep waking one after the other
after another songbird goes rote sublimely.

The heat is unbearable and in near-collapse a fugue state forms.
In it, all love pooled and silver, indistinguishable from a fire tarp
spread cool on the mountain. The light, the heat, it wakes in lasers
contained in an arena of light and in its center:
you, bearing your end points in water.

THESE ARE WHAT I MEAN IN THE DARK CHRISTMASTIME

1___

Poinsettias bloom
the skylined lakeshore.
Small fry scatter
in the unfrozen lake,
afford the water refractive
geometry—green-gold
hexagons netting dead sand.

Moving up through the lattice,
the air ought to shimmer.
Drowned by the line,
back up to where gulls float.
A beach ball as scenery, this horizon's
magnetic, ripples inevitable.

2___

And through it all a promised version of hell never takes shape, which makes it ignorable and worse. An open door, flashing empty above the summertown. I try my best to see it—I know it by the smell, the aura, but to get at it presupposes hunger.

Treading the line, the postponing is pleasant. My lifeboat's battered but the cracks are pluggable. The whirlpool is not, the whirlpool a portal. The whirlpool keeps going with me, my lifeboat and I, stuck in the outer concentrics, plugging leaks.

THERE WERE SIGNS

1___
Of what? Nothing. Maybe death.
The cat choked on a marble.
Is that a sign of death?

2___
Yes. It's also a sign of starvation.
Can you see him in the cemetery?
Yes. I threw up a desert.
Can you see him in the plaster? Yes.

3___
There were signs of abundance. I mean dessert.
There were forty-four bubbles in the resin.
There were a thousand petals on every marigold.
There was a single bat left alive on the coast.

4___
A person should never have woken up this morning.

3___
There was quince paste and figs and brie for brunch.
There were crystal bones scattered on the morning's driveway.

5___
This is what you do: divert your soothsayer.
Give her fifty dollars.

3—
There were silverfish in the bathtub.
There were ants in the rose tea.
There were crows in the chimney.
There were daisies in the field.
There were daisies in the field.

1—
Are these signs of death?
Yes. Collect omens, catalog frequency,
Isolate landscape, cut hair on a full moon.

3—
There were daisies in the field.

6—
Put yourself out there
Into the universe
And wait for the universe
To give you back.

excellent multi-directional read – how did she come up w/ this structure?

HOW IT WORKS

—

Cataclysm science or folding in, a line close
to desperate adventuresome. *Stay here, Scully.*
Casting for horizon, a mind returns dehydrated
but spirited, at least for now. No evidence.
The great river subsides, empires elsewhere.
A path to long life: starved luck, roving Maglite.

—

Cast a line to the Rubicon, fall back. Cast again
from the lack that is you to the world that is
deaf, from the world that is the lack that is
you or not. All the monsters, the flashing lights,
point to *now*. Or, no, but this warning: There is
a planet behind the sun behind a planet behind a sun.
But do we anchor the Milky Way for a minute this year?

—

Trusting, dutiful, here on Earth, you pick
through the chameleon photographs:
index to thumb, index to thumb, blue to orange,
blue to lighter blue, all the time lacking
the transition, incredulity. Blue to orange,
somewhere a threat builds.

—

The time approaches for action. Rather, the action
approaches for time. The black hole yawns, planes fly

themselves, 157 dolphins wash up on the Connecticut shore
while the chameleon still flickers in your hand.
Everything sucks its thumb.

—

Cast for a tracker, a pool of light comes back.
Cast for the coordinates, a flicker, a ping.
Cast for fresh water or poison control.
Cast for a forecast, the coast shrivels up.
Everywhere is Vancouver, everywhere
a forest, and you are always at the brink,
whether you meant to or not.

WESTERN SATELLITE, PILLARS OF CREATION

A daisy field of ne'er-do-wells, tonight a signal burns by
the tracks, edges buttressed, made potent by fire's news.
Cowboy keeper, spreading corrosive—a spell social, otherwhere scant
to the lens, a glint for galaxy. A column blooms cloudy
plume and colorized jet stream for what? For science, for interpreting
the panorama as differentiation from domestic screens, as exceptionalism,
as we got there, as we saw it, wrote it, as genre—or write it bigger,
how we constructed, filmed the narrative, spectacle dazzled it colorized
horizon, brims for ponies or a missing mission grown out of. Stars
are forming. Billows or jets and the sunset bleeds like an dead horse in the fore
-ground—wound we're riding or watching the boundaries split
open to. A tip of the hat, missive, spent hydrogen ultraviolet eats
away at in distance. All of this visually contained, stagnated to a tricky screen still
four light years tall, or a couple thousand miles horizontal in camp
representation, but ought we so easily superimpose the images?

In art, the conflation does not offend though edges suffer.
The bleed becomes a lack and understanding means frozen, or suggestion
of a man, of horse, dead opponent, of feather, that with which to write
a better history told by budget, a film across dead eyes, black fly on iris.
You see, we see, they did. Gravestones as backdrop in field
grass, markers of the dead we still screen as alive.

IN RESPONSE TO POTENTIAL DETRACTORS

If and Since there is no Future or Luck or Fate, I put myself humorously into a coffin. A rocket coffin shaped like a whale in space! No, shaped like a ship, like a whale. I am in a happily receptive state, then—my pieces scattered and bright as confetti.

Shoving off its dock, my coffin and I cut a figure against the sunset. I take a lot of self-portrait action shots of our adventure by holding my cell phone out away from me and smiling. Though the flash erases all behind me, I imagine the message to be still clear.

None other than a nothing vessel, my coffin bobs merrily. Water tests the seams, but I admire the open space where the ceiling once divided the drama from the depths, the audience. Here I see only the walls of the coffin and the sky, churning a charming lavender, now darker.

By the second day spindles take shape in the wood grain. These are neurons and not—

elongated, precise; their pattern indecipherable at this early juncture, but there is, doubtless, a pattern. Thread and dendrites braid themselves forming a raw material any loom worth its warp beam would kill for.

A green flashing starts up and back; my empathy turns cartwheels. My coffin ship weaves a face, one eye flashing. I flash my eye back. I take control of my emotions. I take in the lights.

Where's the shuttle in this light show? It seems now always night out here, adrift—conversations, constellations crossing unaccelerated.

The flashing intensifies—a light to read by in fits and starts, no other colors close. We've no more shuttles. Defunded, components molder. What am I looking at on its own terms out here? The shuttle metals ship to others but forget it, keeping quiet. I press my eye to the coffin wall like a retinal scan. The flashes continue though I swear I heard a click.

—

My battery's died.

—

I've heard the flashing's an instructional aid. I've heard we take control of what we ____, how we ____. Sometimes we work against our better instincts, those resolved in other nerves.

I guess this is a trajectory, but not yet.

HOW TO SINK, HOW TO FIND LIFE

Hello to a broadcast or
Wake for a broadcast—
I forgot, I couldn't
Filter from galaxy knot or
Find the contact, I couldn't
Hear anything at my station.

Emerald ash all rooted
With receptors, ashine
To the core, my center
A valley, bent space
Issues changes like bar codes,
Undersaturated.

I couldn't, a toggle,
I couldn't, the system,
That was my issue last night:
Emission, decree, film, warrant.
Document, you said,
You meant a hairpin, a scalping

I couldn't, keep asking,
Asking everything, it's okay
And you will shout
And you will get it
As your time fills up with more
Different contexts, flowering

Trees, poisoned ice.
Until then, cheer up,
Citizen scientist. Retrieve
Your headset.
The radio waves
Are open

For scan.

CORPOREAL

1 Launch

Hello again, here again with the ghost
ballast, leveling the business of my allegory
with the business of my agency, acting
all in tension. Where skin lapses, where
sun heaves, scouring its edges indecipherable—
this is where blankness settles in for the night.

2 High Tide

I know I'm supposed to keep everything in
mind all at once, but sometimes I live
for my domesticity, tasks accomplished
in a defined series of steps. When I see both
directions simultaneously, I lose my keys and where
are my predecessors then? Where's the collapsing
future global economy arcing back to me as shine,
spotlighting my red plastic key ring, gently
urging me to work on time? My day spent filing.
It's too much, isn't it?

3 Outer Space

I am so glad you never answer, you would be
so disappointed with my lifelong purchasing habits!
This is just a joke: Devour your kind! Errant, pulsing forward:
What's all this shadowy fellow feeling?

What's this propulsion? Are we together in a riverboat?
I do feel I am floating here, autonomy and anatomy at odds.

Ultimately, they say, a trance state
does not hold. Finally, the fallen green
walnuts will blacken and turn soft.
What would happen if I pinned you down?
Red dwarf? Epistolary? Deafness?

4 Wormhole or Whirlpool

A skull full of pens. The center is too
a double. Either the second lives elsewhere,
free of responsibility or the two revolve,
but what's the center then? Or pressed
together to disguise the division?
Why is no one dead where they are
supposed to be? I get there—they're all alive.
It's like a casino in there, signs gestural at best.
Unscrew the ship's navel, all the wagering,
the promises. Everyone's missing limbs
but move like they're forgotten.

5 Dear Dead People:

It's true I can't deal fairly with you, whatever
the reason. I never have. The Lee Shore swoons
away but remains a beckoning vision in my dreams,
first in my waking thoughts. I could say I write

with a well, but really the television's on mute.
I've heard you can hear you in the static.
Is static on television anymore? Will they
bring it back so we can talk or I can listen?

6 Departed Individual Life

I do not scribble my coffin walls,
rather polish a blankness encouraging,
coaxing my mysticism erases, not
ciphers—lazy orthodoxy
to be sure: my troubadour hums only,
taps a finger rhythm on his other wrist—
I rather think his humming better
demonstrates the mystery, better stirs the atoms,
settles the stomach than all the living
words, erasing them sedately—a needful
obsolescence, islands overrun with canals.

Redundant fanaticism, these attacks?
Episodes? A prize? Prismatic, keep paddling.
Purely motored by Fate, I will light a candle
in every night's window in exchange for life
as a happy cog, or shark.

YOU WILL SEE BRILLIANT COLORS

We are located in the tract between
preservation and obsolescence; we are great
vacancies; we are great in our vacancies;
we are fantastic.

Frames of ships that can't but sink sink
and between there's fog; any number of
events associated with the sea.

This is large and also vacant.

When we move hands the hands we see mirror
ways that move the moving in that it and in it
we see hands collecting in movement collections
of seeing mirrors of moving and we move in, we do.

ACKNOWLEDGMENTS AND NOTES

Many thanks to the editors of the following journals, where several of these poems first appeared, sometimes in earlier versions: *TriQuarterly*, *American Letters & Commentary*, *Web Conjunctions*, *Barrow Street*, *Poetry Northwest*, *LVNG*, *Petri Press*, *Heavy Feather Review*, and *Forklift, Ohio*. Some of the poems in this collection also appeared in a chapbook called *We Are Fantastic*, published by Petri Press in 2013.

"Hi! I Am a Machine." borrows the form of its title from the first line of "Negation" by Wallace Stevens. "Cleaning Up the Verbal Situation" borrows its title from the essay "Poetry and Abstract Thought" by Paul Valéry, as translated by Denise Folliet. "Today We're on Vacation" borrows a line from *How to Get Out of the Rat Race and Live on $10 a Month* by George Leonard Herter and Berthe E. Herter. Section IV has a lot to do with *Moby Dick* and *The X Files*.

For reading, time, and kindness: Micah Bateman, Tony Mancus, Katy Chrisler, Montreux Rotholtz, Catherine Blauvelt. Also, of course: Becky Boyle, Molly Boyle, Erika Jo Brown, B.J. Love, Matthew Klane, James Longley, Dan Poppick, Geoffrey Nutter, Alice Fulton, Dan Beachy-Quick. Endless thanks to Nate Pritts, Heidi Reszies, and everyone at H_NGM_N. Thanks also to my family, and lastly, everything all the time: Nate Muthafuckin Brown.

Originally from the Hudson Valley in New York, **THEA BROWN** is a graduate of the Iowa Writers' Workshop, where she was a Truman Capote Fellow. Her poems can be found in *Better*, *The Volta*, *Mississippi Review*, *jubilat*, *TriQuarterly*, *Best New Poets*, and elsewhere. She is the author of the chapbook *We Are Fantastic* (Petri Press) and lives in Baltimore.

H_NGM_N
BOOKS

www.h-ngm-nbks.com

CPSIA information can be obtained at www.ICGtesting.com
Printed in the USA
LVOW11s2157170716

496704LV00004B/115/P